OP

Uau

POCKET POETS SERIES NO. 46

LA LOCA

ADVENTURES ON THE ISLE OF ADOLESCENCE

CITY LIGHTS BOOKS

Some of these poems were published in *The Sierra Madre Review, Endless Party, Inscape, Pretext* (University of Canterbury Literary Review), *City Lights Review Number 2, The Jacaranda Review* (UCLA Literary Quarterly), *Poetry Australia,* and the upcoming anthology from Applezaba Press, *Southern California Arts.* Grateful acknowledgement to producer/animator David Koenigsberg and artist Shawn Kerri for the upcoming animated film version of "Adventures on the Isle of Adolescence."

Library of Congress Cataloging-in-Publication Data

Loca.
    Adventures on the isle of adolescence / by La Loca.
       p. cm. —(Pocket poets series : co. 46)
    ISBN 0-87286-236-4 : $5.95
    I. Title.
    PS3562.0214A67   1989
    811'.54—dc20   89-35426
                                                                CIP

Cover photograph by Peter Milne
Cover design by Rex Ray

City Lights Books are available to bookstores through our primary distributor: Subterranean Company, P. O. Box 168, 265 S. 5th St., Monroe, OR 97456. 503-847-5274. Toll-free orders 800-274-7826. FAX 503-847-6018. Our books are also available through library jobbers and regional distributors. For personal orders and catalogs, please write to City Lights Books, 261 Columbus Avenue, San Francisco, CA 94133.

CITY LIGHTS BOOKS are edited by Lawrence Ferlinghetti and Nancy J. Peters and published at the City Lights Bookstore, 261 Columbus Avenue, San Francisco, CA 94133.

10 9 8 7 6 5 4

In memory of the supreme belletrist
of the American language,
"Miss Orange Grove" 1949:
Ann Sanchez-Whitaker

*"The sick think they are well,
and the well think they are sick."*

I am indebted to many, many people; here are some of those who have guided me. My professor and mentor, Ron Koertge; and poets Darrell Vienna, Ivan Morley, Theresa Thalken, Jan Ueber and Leslie Monsour in the workshop, geniuses all. Poets Jack Foley, Trevor Carolan, John Tranter, John Millett, Robert Peters, Paul Trachtenberg, Kai Jensen and Wanda Coleman. Lorenzo, Sr., Nancy Peters, Bob Sharrard, and special love to my editor, Amy Scholder, at City Lights Books. Charles Champlin and Itabari Njeri of the *Los Angeles Times*. My mega-agent, Paul Alan Smith of Triad. Radio stations CKLN (Toronto), CO-OP (Vancouver), WFMU (New York), WUSB (Long Island), The Germ at KUSF (San Francisco), KXLU (Los Angeles), and 2JJJ (Sydney). Filmmakers Claudia Bryant and Sophie Rachmuhl. The Watts of San Pedro, and Rich Bruland of Be Bop. And my thanks to my adored friends, the two Bonnies, Dr. Myra, Dr. Marta, Dr. Alice, Roberta, Candace, Bill & Lenore, Susan Kamei, Mrs. Doris Siegel, D. Wanker, Deb Jordan & Deb Kagan, Candy Azarra, Pat Winter, Gina, Cathy, Stella, Rachelle and Claudette and Dr. Leo Rubinstein. The doctors who saved my life: Ronald Leuchter and Howard Mandel. And mostly, my beloved grandmother, Mrs. Henrietta Hyman Berney, who died as this book went to press.

Photo by Rod Rolle

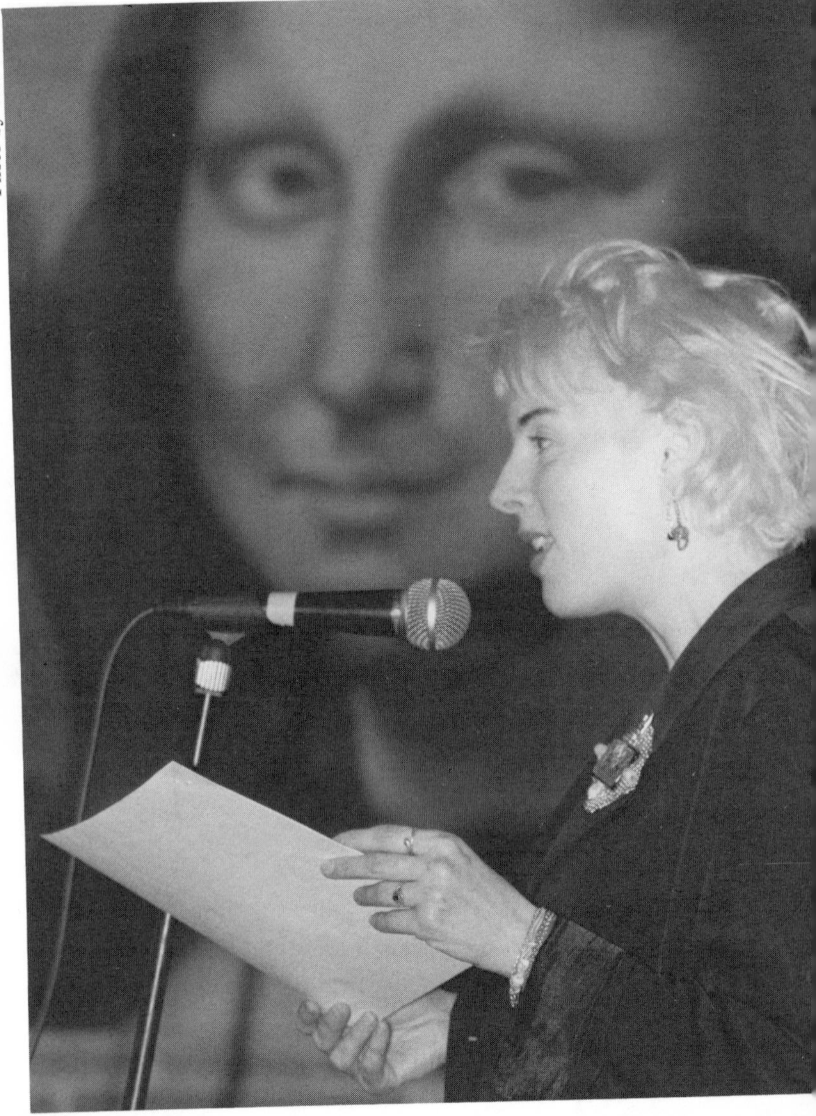

WAR

Red Sun
over Echo Park
orbiting
an unheard-of botany
of disfigured statues
sprung never far from
the twig.
Underneath this fig leaf
my mother became an atheist.

A persimmon's throw from Black Monday
were the clack of the trolleys
the stomp of the Lindy
the crackle of zootsuiters spindling reefers
the pixilated palms
the plump Temple
& you
made in the image of
banana curls, leviathan dimples
& empires hemmed at the Veneris.
You
in the baked brick ice box
the one room
where you lived your whole life

with delivered milk
where your mother rose at 5 A.M.
and your father was a handyman.
How did you touch yourself
I wonder
in a room
crowded with
their separation
and your dream
of aquatic ballet?

You all kept your volcanos quiet
during the blackout
while you lay still
waiting for the hum
of the kamikazes.

Outside
the patriotic wore their designations:
I Am Chinese.

Inside
the world was made safe
for your mother
to work long hours
as a janitor in the annihilation industry.
She wore duck coveralls.

Your father,
too old to be conscripted,
conscripted you.
He did you up in his contumely;
his belittlement of you
in the one dress you owned
and how stupid you were.
His round eyes grew rounder
at the sight of his spitting image
biting her fingernails
in the ditch of Eden.
And you said to him,
"Am I going to be blown up?"

Down swept the sky with talons
with its jowls, with its beard
with its red bull's eye
and its impregnating pupil:
"Let me show you what a man is!"
Echo Park fell
and a scientist has the right
to insert his tongue
into the mouth
of any child.
Hands for blades;
fingers: incisors;
he strapped you,

in the extinction position,
to his table of ablation.
It was over in a minute.
Your swimming pool in pieces in the sky.
Your obedience to the
hydrophobe who got you
in the kitchen.
He made legs out of you.
The bomb,
with the mousetrap in its womb,
delivered.
Your backstroke in the Milky Way,
Your life jacket of morbidity,
Your nipples,
all puerile and all thumbs:
a fresh white flag
hung in the middle of the wish for death.
"Good Morning, Mr. & Mrs. America.
This morning, at 8:15 A.M.,
In Hiroshima, an industrial city
Fifteen hundred miles southwest of Tokyo
140,000
Japanese. . .Japanese. . .Japanese. . .Japanese. . ."

Your mother came home, fatigued.
She pulled off her boots
and tied on an apron.
A pin dropped.

And you could hear
Krakatoa
as far away as
the sun.

DRAGON MAN

You are a witch,
Your spoor of jack-o'-lanterns and smithies
suffocates my will to do better in life
and
I want to be reptilian and dangerous
as you
are
now.
Can it be
Your flesh is unguent to this scorching October
but
Your build burns
You stoke and salve together
If you don't stop
I will die of smoke inhalation.

Lying with noses pressed together:
I breathe your breath of pyromanic myrrh.
Dragon man, don't get so overheated
Your groin is crumbling
leaves incinerating in Autumn
You rosin your tongue with viper's sarsaparilla
Every guy oughtta have a
chimney
and
the smell of your Lucky Strikes.

THINKING OF YOU FROM THE BEACH

Pimp sun & pimp beers,
the scent of fish,
and all day asking:
"What do mailboxes look like
in Algarve?"
Noon
is a postcard from Portugal.
The lambent sands of Falesia
as remote and molten
as your stylo:
"Hi there!
How's your poetry?
Hope your health is improving!
Say 'Hi' to Charles!
Take care, your friend . . ."

". . . P.S. How are the younger men! . . ."

Nobody on earth
believes in sandcastles anymore
but I could wait for a boy
who wished me there in
a hot cove and
the face of Maria da Gloria

and then
signed his name.

This is an aerial age.
No bare feet.
Sun worshippers
have been arguing
from the beginning that
smashing atoms
solves long distances
so never again will we have to
misunderstand and die.
Communication is a physical act.
In my hand I hold a beach
where you could make love
in the open.
In a conch
you can hear
the first amphibian
choose land forever.
In your scrawl
I'm oiling
in the sweat from
your red chest.

I RECEIVED THIS WOMAN'S INTIMACIES

Visiting my ex-lover's mother's house
three days after his father's passing.
The overstuffed hasn't been told yet.
John Wayne's re-runs still stare
in the direction
of the master of the house,
ghost to ghost.
She's seated in his thick absence
as much monogrammed
as his lighter and flannel.

I sit where I always sat
when I was his son's girl
way at the end of his longevity
while he lit up
and told me stories of his mistresses.

But on the back porch
the mother told me
that she had no vagina
and her husband had no prostate
these had been removed to
extend their lives

while in the living room
the father was a monsoon puffing Shermans
and the son entranced in Time
sitting an end table apart
in matching swivels
battling to the death
to be
impersonal.

Ah, but we were lovers
and I filled the ears of the man of the house
full of his son's orgasm.
I was not what they wanted for him.
But it was the fire season
and their saber-toothed brawls with their boy
over leaving dirty creamers in the sink
were in weed,
dry,
waiting for a match.

We were always in bed
above the old couple below,
with their remote controls.
Always, always I could hear
her fear of her husband's heart
while he turned red and crazy
and dragged the bronco-buster from the nicotine,

let it ride him
let the smoke writhe
up,
blazing the beamed nave,
infusing the coil springs of the son's squander.
I will never leave you,
said the men.

She needs to tell me.
She needs to tell me about the
drive to Palomar
in his Dad's Excelsior.
How he wore his black wetsuit.
How he held his father in his hands,
immersed in the Pacific.
How he touched his father.
It was hard to hear the ex-Marine
in the wisps.
How, quivering fingers
through the might
the loud glance
the full head of hair,
clutchful after clutchful
he flew his father's ire on the surf.
How she stood on the shore
watching her husband's remains
empty the urn

with the beautiful long fingers
she once married.

She loses control
and I let her.
She's frail
in the doomful concavity of his overstuffed,
his freshly opened half-a-pack and his digitalis
at her elbow. Without even thinking
she closes the lid on the box.
I count the widows.

YOU SHOULD ONLY GIVE HEAD
TO GUYS YOU REALLY LIKE

Hush
Pharoah in death
Bloodless
The priests' prayers are finished
The eyes of your soul meet mine
I enter your bedroom
By summon
To lead you
through the avenues of afterlife
into Heaven.

Oh God! You are so sexy
You are doing your levitation act
On linens
Caulked and malted with the
Balm and stuff
Undertakers love
And you are levitating
Nude
Lank and improper
With the threat of nirvana.

Oh Christ! You are so sexy
I stand a Sphinx

Mortared in a body of stone
Rock talons silting at the lapping spit of the Nile.
You are the East
And I cannot move my unmuscled mass
Toward a theory.
I am mind and you are man.
And your soul's eyelashes
are long
and
pretty.

Oh, I love that
Killed king
Across the Nile.
My brick shrinks to flesh
I lass-like vault
from my monumental crouch
and fall into the river
a woman

And I move toward you
Thighs folding 'neath a stale slip
cutting the Nile
Bashed westerly by stabbing waters
But I inch East
on human toes
To your windlessness.

You are nuder and closer
and the faint scent of summer orange
from your airless tomb
keeps me starting eastward
In this wet midnight.

Sire
I enter your sarcophagus, dripping.
I have brought your lost life
an apple, magic, and a freshly starched shirt.
I shoo death away.
It cannot argue because it is
Nothingness
and I am
Pola Negri.

Soul! C'mere.
These incarnations were all hieroglyph.
Now, quiver, like life.
I touch you

and there is a tumult in Cairo.
Heady with grave robbing
Heady with necromancy
Heady with the mead of sweat on your scrotum
I swipe a saxophone from the atomic age
And with goddess kisses on the reed

Suck you.
Death is deaf
but not me
I'm going to suck your dick to saxophones
And get a crush on when you come.

Your breath is on Venus
Your heart is in a back alley

Your soul penetrates your body.

Cramp, cord
Roused
The bed's muslin
scratches you aware
of
Hands gloving your groin
And your cock like a deep vowel. . .

Hush!
You Are
So Sexy!

you are so sweetly sexy.
One simple tremble
And I fall in love with you again
Sigh or choke

And I fall in love with you again
Wallow or lean this way or that
And I fall in love with you again

And now
The taste that flirts upon my tongue
As you send your carrier pigeon to Egypt
A second, drought
Then the Nile
and then
      my flooding mind.

Your orb, scepter and crown, restored
You sit
You stand
You banish me back to the West
Where I will creak on my haunch
Until the next time
My riddles and my antiquity
murder you
and you
Summon.

VA BAISER TA CHÈVRE

. . . Pigalle, 1971

She was the oldest woman
in the line
of cloven feet.
Part pigeon-toed
mini-skirted
with legs bowed like a throat
she looked like the kind of woman
you could ask to urinate on you.

O, yes, I was a true *intellectuelle*
in the front seat
of a back seat
with my two Frogs
practicing my French.
My greenhorn, my hot pants and my Hallwag's,
in a guzzling Chevrolet,
touring the Europeans behind the windshield.
Mon Dieu! Sacrebleu! I had the cramps.
Oui, Oui, Paris, the city of existentialism
where I lived cheaply
in the room of a maid
consuming Feta, *Gauloises* and sperm.
I was a *vraie bluestocking.*
The flood of Bloody Mary's

diked by an Athenian diaphragm,
I was so drunk
I didn't know the men I was with
so I named them *Homo sapiens*.
Homo sapiens the driver
had an erection
nearly grazing his goatee
and every finger of my hand was like a genital.
Homo sapiens the passenger
had me as a passenger
exhibiting my mastery of declension,
phlebotomizing all over his crotch.
"Un Tampax, s'il vous plaît!!!!
Est-ce que quelqu'un a un Tampax par ici?"
Le pauvre Homo sapiens begged of every passing *fille*.

I'd never had an orgasm
Not even in my multiple nudities
not even when I got a nose ring
not even on hashish and barbituates in the sewers
on the boat
with the docent
who was blond and polyglot
and picked me from the
prettier Americans
because my teeth were crooked
because the corn belt girls

said *"faire l'amour, faire l'amour"*
and I said
"Take me, and I will thrust my tongue into your rectum."

She knew.
She-god of widowed palms
with fifty years of blunt eyes
and omniscience.
She knew what separated the human female
from the chill of silver.
The rabbit's foot she'd kept for sterility;
her heart of cement,
and how she came to be the carrier of explosions.
Like hell
it hurt
but she spent the whole night
shifting from one foot to the other.

"Hey, Grandma!"
howled *Homo sapiens*,
"How much are you?"

RELATIONS

I only knew them with their clothes on.
My mother wore tight leopard-spot capris,
belted, with her shirt tucked in
to show off her flat stomach.

In her brand-new husband's old Thunderbird
I crawled onto the shelf
behind the buckets of tuck 'n roll
fitting myself between the cold glass
and the necks of the newlyweds.
I would barely breathe.
In the two hours to Arcadia
in the matter of urination
it was customary
for me to raise my hand.

We arrived with our trunk full
of Fritos.
Ruth and Eddie were our
only relations
who had a back yard.
The grass was white and crackled.
It had been trampled
by Ruth's eight children

and by shopping carts
because Eddie was a shopping cart repairman.
Just like last year
Eddie wore a tie
and had just returned from Las Vegas.
Just like last year
the swing set had chains
but no seats
and there was that big motorboat
called "Soul Captain"
blocking the driveway
hitched to a waterspout
ever since I could remember.
Just like last year
all the cousins got together
browning burgers and splitting bagels
with smiles
and a new set of spouses.

My grandmother and her two sisters
were sewing machine operators
at a Mafia-run bra factory
in Hollywood.
They presided over the card tables
and the metal folding chairs.
All the men had curly hair
and the women wore rollers to bed.

"Potato salad makes your hair curly"
two old women admonished me
about something I hated.
They bulged out of their sack dresses
& tested the mettle of the
poker chairs.

Inside the house
the tribesmen huddled
booing a pigskin

while nearby
in a cross-hatched playpen
two unrelated babies
had been placed together.
"Jackie, say 'hello' to your third cousin Ray's
new wife's baby from a former marriage, Larry."
And Jackie sized him up
drooled
wee-weed
and crawled across the prescribed turf
of formulae and teething rings
to little Larry
and socked him good.

Outside
the Tupperware had lost its pink.

The women were assembled
around the battered pans
dishing chopped liver.
I adored the feel of my mother's body
under the plump sun
as we sat side by side
sharing a chair.
She was the only one
at the table
with red hair.
I munched deviled eggs
in cadence to "vasectomies," "divorce,"
and "Huh! Really! That bastard!"
and I preened
as my mother touched me and touched me.

Back in the back of the T-bird
I waved "good-bye."
All the way home
my mother triumphed
at how fat her cousin Ruth was
who ten years ago
had left her oldest
in an orphanage
to run off
on the back of a motorcycle
with a shower door installer.

"You can tell she's a whore from her stomach,"
my mother said.
"Did you see her big stomach?
Women with bellies are compelled
to give in
to men."

EXOMOLOGESIS

I

I don't usually get myself
into these situations.
His bedroom is a catacomb.
There is a poster of Farrah Fawcett.
There is the playmate of July.
There is his fiancée
her face framed in wrought iron atop
his pine bureau
as if beheaded.
He wears an executioner's hood
as he is naked
and comes into his
bed of nails
and reaches for me.
Nothing in his bedroom nay-says
but his fiancée's farsighted eyes.
I do not thank him.
Beneath shrouds and shrouds of
history
at the spiral
he dreams of

slicing somebody's white neck.
I'll live as long as I'm myopic
so I remain objective.
He's stabbing Miss July
real good.
His body becomes a metronome
It's bloody
and her scream is making a mess
so he pulls out her vocal chords
and cuts them.
What a hell of an orgasm!
And me,
I'm as still
as a still
of a nude
woman.

II

I'm never gonna get myself into
this situation again
so long as I live.
But he's soft
with sheepskins and melon lavalieres
and I do my very best not to drop a drop
of my whisky on his eyelet spread.

He's built like a woman
and is ashamed
but he unlaces his shoes
because he wants me.
He departs his
crocheted coverlets and pianos
to kiss my slipper.
I hide in a whole
bottle of Seagram's.
The lights are out
but my gall is lucid.
It's best this way,
for a terrified man & a terrified woman
to be
Shocked
and I know
the girl he's cheating on is homely
and I know
he stutters stale impurities
sneaked from filthy books because
his own are too awful
and I know
he wants to be good, bad
and I know
I drank for obfuscation
not this unsparing
eye

and God I know
it isn't nice for me to stare
but I stare:

> *Oh Don't Love Me Don't Love Me Jesus*
> *Why Do You Have To Love Me For A*
> *Few Moments of Ill-gotten Compassion?*

And in a few moments when
I feel,
when on my thigh I feel
his scrawny penis hard again,
I understand that understanding
is not a
prophylactic.

III

Why do I always get myself
into these situations?
We love like man and wife
for hours.
I've waited so long for a
chance to be in his bed.
I wore red dresses, White Shoulders,
and sent him origamis
of myself
so I could be here.

I knew his cock would
be as handsome as his brown eyes
and the way he calls me
lover.
I come like a bride.
More hours.
I fuck him as if
to rip his body away
from anything that
interferes,
even his own mind.
Especially that.
It's hard to love without rage.
I wrap myself in his
red, red hours
and seduce him all I
want.
I pray to my flesh to please
remember.
He won't.
I step out of bed,
flush with sex,
and pull on his wife's
cerise kimono.

WHY I CHOOSE BLACK MEN FOR MY LOVERS

Acid today
is trendy entertainment
but in 1967
Eating it was eucharistic
       and made us fully visionary

My girlfriend and I used to get cranked up
       and we'd land in
       The Haight
       and oh yeah
       The Black Guys Knew Who We Were
       But the white boys
       were stupid

I started out in San Fernando
       My unmarried mother did not abort me
       because Tijuana was unaffordable
       They stuffed me in a crib of invisibility
       I was bottle-fed germicides and aspirin
       My nannies were cathode tubes
       I reached adolescence, anyway
       Thanks to Bandini and sprinklers

In 1967 I stepped through a windowpane
        and I got real
        I saw Mother Earth and Big Brother
        and
        I clipped my roots which choked in the
                concrete
                of Sunset Boulevard
        to go with my girlfriend
        from Berkeley to San Francisco
        hitchhiking
        and we discovered
        that Spades were groovy
        and
        White boys were mass-produced and
        watered their lawns
                artificially with long green hoses in
                West L.A.

There I was, in Avalon Ballroom
        in vintage pink satin, buckskin and
                patchouli,
                pioneering the sexual
                revolution
I used to be the satyr's moll, half-woman,
and the pink satin hung
        loose about me
        like an intention

I ate lysergic for breakfast, lunch and
          dinner
     I was a dead-end in the off-limits of
          The Establishment
          and morality was open to interpretation

In my neighborhood, if you fucked around, you were a whore

But I was an émigrée, now
     I watched the planeloads of white boys fly
          up from Hamilton High
     They were the vanguard
          of the Revolution
     They stepped off the plane
          in threadbare work shirts
          with rolled-up sleeves
          and a Shell Oil, a Bankamericard,
          a Mastercharge in their back pocket
          with their father's name on it
     Planeloads of Revolutionaries
     For matins, they quoted Marcuse and Huey Newton
     For vespers, they instructed young girls from
          San Fernando to
          Fuck Everybody
     To not comply, was fascist
I watched the planeloads of white boys
          fly up from Hamilton High

All the boys from my high school were shipped to
      Vietnam
And I was in Berkeley, screwing little white boys
      who were remonstrating for peace
        In bed, the pusillanimous hands of war protestors
          taught me Marxist philosophy:
        Our neighborhoods are a life sentence
        This was their balling stage and they
          were politicians
        I was an apparition with orifices
        I knew they were insurance salesmen in their
          hearts
        And they would all die of attacks
        I went down on them anyway, because I had
          consciousness
        Verified by my intake of acid
        I was no peasant!
        I went down on little white boys and
        they filled my head with
          Communism
        They informed me that poor people didn't have
          money and were oppressed
        Some people were Black and Chicano
        Some women even had illegitimate children
        Meanwhile, my thighs were bloodthirsty
          whelps
        and could never get enough of anything

and those little communists were stingy
I was seventeen
       and wanted to see the world
       My flowering was chemical
       I cut my teeth on promiscuity and medicine
       I stepped through more windowpanes
           and it really got oracular
In 1968
One night
The shaman laid some holy shit on me and wow
I knew
in 1985
       The world would still be white, germicidally
           white
       That the ethos of affluence
       was an indelible
       white boy trait
       like blue eyes
       That Volkswagons would be traded in for
           Ferraris
           and would be driven with the same
           snotty pluck that sniveled around
           the doors of Fillmore, looking cool
I knew those guys, I knew them when they had posters of
       Che Guevara over their bed
       They all had posters of Che Guevara over
           their bed

And I looked into Che's black eyes all
        night while I lay in those beds,
        ignored
Now these guys have names on doors on the 18th floor of
        towers in Encino
        They have ex-wives and dope connections.
Even my girlfriend married a condo-owner in Van Nuys.

In proper white Marxist theoretician nomenclature, I was
        a tramp.
The rich girls were called "liberated."

I was a female from San Fernando
        and the San Francisco Black Men and I
        had a lot in common
        Eyes, for example
        dilated
        with the opacity of "fuck you"
        I saw them and they saw me
        We didn't need an ophthalmologist to get it on
        We laid each other on a foundation of
            visibility
        and our fuck
        was no hypothesis

Now that I was worldly
        I wanted to correct

the nervous blue eyes who flew up from
Brentwood
to see Hendrix
but
when I stared into them
They always lost focus
and got lighter and lighter
and
No wonder Malcolm called them Devils.

GENESIS

I grew up in a house
where the matriarch
hung her rancid panties
over a doorknob
in the vestibule,
crotch out.

So is it any wonder
I ended up so
unbosoming?
And you see that's why
when he said
his girlfriend
would be home from
cocktail waitressing in 15 minutes
so we had to screw quick
on the slaughtered zebra's skin in the hallway
very immaculately
so as not to leave coccyx impressions
I said
"You bet!"

& when we did it
the only illumination

was a 50-lb. sea bottom
she gave him,
with a pump
& a chain:
horses & weed
pink hobnailed ticklers
lichen, nautili and squid.
How strange, I thought,
how cruel,
just one of each kind,
no mates.

A BRIEF ENCOUNTER

My grandmother
ceremoniously devoured
the obituaries
every morning
while she sucked quartered lemons to the peel.
Fifty-three years after divorcing him
she saw his curt paragraph
between a Hula dancer
and a Cantonese mortician.
She spit the pips
on a Melmac saucer
like a sovereign,
folded the Metro section
and later
rolled it
and caused it
to exterminate a fly.

ADVENTURES ON THE ISLE
OF ADOLESCENCE

Hello, animal sacrifice hotline?
Do you incinerate teenage boys?
Here they come
The Swarm
Hear the drone of their skateboards
As they approach
like an armada
and run
for cover of the nearest sleazy bar
where they check I.D.
and have bouncers like rhinoceri
Secrete thyself on the furthest stool
Shield thyself with a vodka martini
and wait till the air raid siren ceases.
17 years ago
polite company
screwed on hallucinogens
with the intent to produce
offspring which would be
trippy.
This coup of genetic engineering —
enacted at Be-ins, under bushes, on acid —
was to be the Aquarian gift to the race.
After all, by 1961

God's remains had been discovered in a
tar pit by the County Museum.
He was dead.
Laboratories were Lord
and Chemistry was Life.
Junkies and alkies slouched the earth
Supreme.
And the brain damaged naturally selected the
brain damaged
and they were born
incubated on fungus and fry
yanked from the host
buzzed like a saw.
The Scions of Altered Consciousness.
The New Breed.
And now
the population is overrun with the little
aberrations.
And the little aberrations are so huge.
Bigger than me.
Dinosaurian!
Come to find out
Prenatal dosages of
lysergic and tetrahydrocannabinol
induce giantism and
increased production of androgen
and here they come again

The Master Race
Flowing in a fleet
a platoon
the hellish sibilance of metal crushing concrete
and
The pack veering toward me in formation
like I'm quarry.
I'll just keep walking down the sidewalk
like I don't notice
the juggernaut of testosterone
mowing me down.
I grip my purse to me, tight
with the angst that only those in
majority can know and
I pray to the God who was reinstated
in 1979:
Please
let this be the primarily peyote-gestated branch
which rarely bites
Please
let them be crocked on
popsicles, Coors and cheap Mexican weed
Please, please
just let me get to the end of the block
without getting a chunk of my butt
tweaked by a twit
and they thrash by

thunderous
in a deafening brouhaha
with a mighty "fuck this" and
a mighty "fuck that"
Fuck biology
Fuck trigonometry
Fuck those PDAP meetings my old man makes me go to
Fuck the cops
Fuck Reagan
Fuck Deukmejian
Fuck Felicia that trendy twat with her fat-assed sister
Fuck Madonna
Fuck Heavy Metallers
Fuck Death Rockers
Fuck Punks
Fuck Trendies
Fuck Stoners
Fuck everybody everywhere in the entire world
all the time for any reason.
A congested aggregate of gnats
dense with fuck
and they slalom around me
and I only get goosed once.
Thank you God.
There is a God.
I take a deep breath.

This is adolescence:
Your world has four corners
and folds up neatly
and fits in your pants' pocket
— There goes a marsupial now! —
You can put it in your pocket
and there's room left over for
cherry bombs and Marlboros
Your mother launders it every weekend
You can dirty it and leave it lying around
and she'll wash it again for free
and you can fold it and stuff it
and mount on your little
island
and be Icarus all you want.
But when you're of the age of reason
the world is no longer flat
it has no edge
it boggles Daedalus
and it wrinkles
but you can't grasp it
can't clean it
can't trade it
can't bear it
but you are in it, forever
whether you get high or not.

Uh oh.
Aforementioned marsupial
has whipped around on the back
of his skateboard
wheels, professionally
to flash me some prowess, I would imagine
and he considers me
like a Doberman homicidally scenting
an interloper.
He moves toward me
all fours spinning
activated by his olfactory and his thalamus
and he uninvited
attaches himself to my person
like an aphid
with an obtrusion.
I, the adult,
have a superego
which enjoins
that such casual encounters between a marsupial
of fifteen
and a respected, educated, self-supporting,
world-traveled, condo-owning urbane woman
of thirty-six
are merely formalities to communicate
innocent ephemera:
Directions, The Time, Got A Match? and

other banalities of everyday existence
which strangers the world o'er frequently
impart to one another on the street without
incurring penitentiary sentences.
"Excuse me," he says, without spitting,
"Weren't you at 3 Dollar Cuts
last Tuesday?"
Where did he learn such obvious intros,
from his elders?
3 Dollar Cuts? Me, at 3 Dollar Cuts?
This snaky misdemeanant thinks he's
gonna make me a felon.
"Why, yes. As a matter of fact, I was at
3 Dollar Cuts last Tuesday. Your skateboard
does look familiar. It's such a nice one.
Little turquoisy emblems and things. I'd
spot it anywhere."
"I'm Todd." He thrusts
me his hand, big as a man's.
It's covered with inked cabala,
cuts, scabs, scarifications and immolations
of all natures; pussy, infected, bleeding
things, meticulously inflicted.
I take it
and
die
in his palm.

He tells me about the
Echo and the Bunnymen concert
the Dead Kennedys, Crass
and his Steel Pulse collection.
His mother's got a new boyfriend and
he can't sleep at night
because her wails waken him
and at breakfast he delivers commentaries
to her and her lover about their
vigor.
His dad's an asshole who dealt
drugs when he was a hippie but now he's
a stockbroker and a hypocrite with a house in
Sherman Oaks and his new stepmother's a cunt.
She's thirty and thinks she's his mother and
two weeks after she married his dad she hit him
so he hit her back and she flew across the
room and incurred a concussion and his dad
came in and threatened his life.
Together, the two of them rag on him about
his dirty room, his lazy friends, his drug
habits and his truancy. For his birthday, they're
getting him an electric guitar. Last summer he
worked for his Uncle Norm and has enough money
saved to get maybe an '81 Ford when he's sixteen.
His dad used to take him to a dry pool
at an abandoned estate

and he'd skateboard for hours in the
deep end
while his dad would sit on a bench
reading *Moby Dick*
and half of his class came home with
him during lunch hour and they had
a bomb in the living room and the
Guatemalan maid came in
and threw them out with
earsplitting Spanish and a broom
and last summer he was dating
Wendy Loper and they'd stay out all
night going pool-hopping in Tarzana
and once he pinned his mother
against the refrigerator door with
a knife at her throat
and how do I like his new creepers?
He pants around the stretch of his
universe with the finish line
here at my feet.
His feet are nailed to his board,
two inches above earth,
scaffolding lordliness.
He has run out of tin soldiers
and Dodger cards.
We are just two people.
His eyes are hazel.

He sputters into some
frothy loquacity about how his
mom's salsa is jesus
and it's only because I wanted to
go to bed with something clean
I wanted the lights out
and I wanted to be a Rorschach
wooed by eyes that see in the dark
and because Aphrodite is an eidetic girl
and because we'd make love
           like unscrabbling a rebus
whispering into unbathed ears
           the things we got
and because it's the Ice Age
and he'd roll me up in him
           like a Saskatchewan pelt
so no bad winter can come in and molest
me *ever*
"Ocupado!" I'll taunt at Chronos, "Ocupado!"
and because no one had asked me out
           for six months
and because
it's the noblesse oblige of
the female to be
nice
I said:
"TODD."

Todd froze, mid-consonant.
"Why don't I give you my phone number
and we can continue this conversation
tonight."

*   *   *   *   *   *

Tacoland.
Three beef & bean burritos
two cheese enchiladas
five tacos
three mexiburgers
a fries
an apple turnover
and a Michelob
we dissembled was for me
and for which I got
demonstrably
carded.
(There is a God).
As for me
just a diet soda, thank you.
I didn't want to impinge too ruthlessly
on his
allowance.
(Not on the first date).
He doesn't force the issue.
"My mom diets, too."
And he pulls a fat wad of

twenties out of his front pocket.
For that, he can carry the entire
tray with my diet soda on it
himself.
I move off to the table of choice
and he stops me, saying
"Gotta pee!"
and he skateboards out the entrance
to the parking lot
leaving me with thirty-five pounds
of his hoage.

There we are, the natty couple.
He's an emaciated six feet
and probably weighs
two pounds less
than my rotund five foot four.
He heaps down his burgers,
slobbers his jalapeños,
guzzles his Michelob
and belches just to let me know he can.
He smears the excess around his mouth
with the back of his hand.
He smiles at me, a happy boor
perfectly aware that he's
meticulously disgusting.
He plies his palate with tacos

like a manual laborer,
flicks his hair out of his eyes
goes to it with relish
tongue and fingers actively engaged
efficient and uninhibited.
When I think of all those years
trying to shame those Tom Selleck types
into giving me head —
Won't be a problem here!
I wonder how I can get him to
wash his hands?
I'll put Boraxo on the night stand
next to the Crisco!
He'll sit on the edge of my bed
and stare at the alien paraphernalia
suspiciously trying to
hide his perplexity
and then he'll say something epiphanic like:
"My mom uses Crisco to cook."
And I'll pat his little hand and reassure him,
"So do I."

"So, Todd,
tell me about the tenth grade."
So he tells me.
And it's another recitation of
trivia

that wears on my sensibilities.
He goes back to order seconds.
He goes back to order thirds.
The patience in my diet soda has
melted.
And he's in the middle of
some exuberant account of how
he and Jason stole an '81 Cougar
in broad daylight, drove it to
Malibu, wiped the fingerprints off
it and abandoned it and got
away with it and ha, ha, ha . . .
All I wanted to do was spank him
and order him to pick up his room.
I wanted a little white apron.
Oh, no, this is weird. This is
really getting weird. Give me
Tom Selleck, I don't care.
I stood up.
"TODD. Stop. Just stop. That's
enough. I don't want to know anymore.
And furthermore Todd, the
date is over. End of date."
Todd jumped up. He dropped his
mexiburger on the floor. Before my
own eyes he pulled a paper napkin out of
the napkin holder and wiped both his

hands and his mouth. And it almost
broke my heart the way he pleaded,
"Don't you wanna go to the movies?"
"Todd, si' down."
We sat back down. He folded his
hands on his lap.
"Todd, don't fold your hands on your
lap. Put them on the Formica table top
and drum them nervously. That's a
good boy. Look, Todd, I don't want
you to take this personally, okay? Don't
take this personally. I hate teenage boys.
I hate them! I want to incinerate all
of them. I want to ship them off to
wars. I want to support Reagan. I shouldn't
but I do. I mean, let me tell you
about adolescence. I'm gonna tell you
about adolescence. I'm gonna tell
you about the tenth grade.
Being adolescent is like being born
in the caves
in pithecanthropica
and waking up one day on a skateboard
on Rodeo Drive at high noon
with braces and funnies and a tire iron
& a T-shirt that says
Eat Shit.

Don't take this personally, Todd
but your mind is still in the tar pits
with a profound paleolithic mysticism
requiring human sacrifice
and of which you aspire to be
the most fanatical exponent.
Don't take this personally, Todd
Innocent people walk by you with nothing
but Mastercharges
O boy, wait till the guys back in the tribe
hear about this!
You figure a little dismemberment and cannibalism
is all part of your rite of initiation
'cause you know the shaman sent you here
so you can slaughter up a storm
and go back and get your badge
calligraphied on your face — to match
your hand.
Don't take this personally, Todd
But the trouble with you troglodytes is
you're so doctrinaire.
I know it's called "graffiti"
You know what graffiti is?
I'll tell you what graffiti is:
messy arabesques of the jingoist illiterati
garbled fetishistic codices of the raving mad
blotchy illuminations of lunacy

— Don't take this personally, Todd —
littering hieroglyphic excretions
wanton, anti-syntactical harebrain cryptograms
iconographic scribblings of regressive smut
ugly ideograms of idiocy
and
totems of brio and death wish
That's graffiti.
Have you no lexicon!
Even the vandal himself is awed.
Don't take this personally, Todd
But you're Huns
Huns marauding megalopolis
demanding we hand over our ghetto blasters.
I know the putsch of libido in the smashing glass
of a beer bottle.
It's mysticism.
Don't tell me it's rage
or Robert Rauschenberg
It's mysticism.
Mysticism!
And this is the
phenomenology of the glands.
Oh, Todd, I can tell you're taking
this personally. Don't take this
personally, Todd, but I can prove that
it's mysticism because you've got

Muezzins!
Muezzins
with their larynx in their prostate
vavooming by in cars like burning bushes
squealing nonobjective scatalogical revelations
at me
like I'm Mecca.
Muezzins and more muezzins.
In a palladium of acolytes
muezzins at the microphone
sacerdotally ululating fortississimo
nasty glossolalia
way amped
to spay psyche and
make gonads vatic.
Tell me that's not mysticism —
Go on, I dare you!
And it's only because I'm a
philologist
that when attending one of your services
that I can even hang.
Todd, don't personalize this, don't!
But when exegetes,
such as myself,
carefully interpret
the xenoglotted squalls
hooliganistic shibboleths

and earsplitting hierograms
wailed to the faithful,
it isn't
mean heathen fry-brain dadaism: "Life Sucks."
Not even.
Suicide is noble.
No.
It's the cosmology of snot:
PISS OFF!
Is that a mantra, or what?
Now, Todd, I can tell you're
taking this very personally, but
You lie. YOU LIE.
And you know that you lie.
But you don't lie the way men lie:
psychopathically.
"When will I see you again?"
"Soon."
No, you fib, like rough puppies:
"I'm just gonna leave here
and then stop by Corey's
and get my Red Lorry, Yellow Lorry
album and then pick up a Hershey Bar,
and then stop by Joshua's to score
some hash I've heard he's got and then
I'm gonna party for an hour and then
I'm just gonna do my American History

homework and then I'll
call
you
up."
I can't suffer to be
tête à tête with such shit.
You think this is a date?
This was never a date!
There's supposed to be some
tender liturgy to a date
The dinner
The movie
and the thereafter
when your gentility is the
duenna
and your imagination the
cicerone . . .
You think I'm a parking lot, don't you.
Oh, how can you expect savoir faire
from Siva the Destroyer.
Okay, I don't want savoir faire.
I relinquish savoir faire.
There it goes. Begone!
Todd, couldn't you drag me off Alley Oop style?
Take me to the milk-and-cookie land of stupidity?
It's a pyrrhic victory
to have lived as long as I.

I wanna lose.
Outright lose.
Enlightenment isn't cute.
I've had my reasons for living
disemboweled alive.
See, Prometheus was a woman.
She was university educated but she
slept with a lot of vultures.
So, I can't run off with a cave painter now!"
A Salvadorian came
to our table. He took away
the cold burritos which
had not been touched.
Todd cupped my hand in his own.
"So I'm young, so? So?
Doesn't make any difference to me.
Besides, maturity is sexy."
"It is?????"
"Damn straight! And besides, I think
you look great."
"I do?????"
"As a matter of fact, my mom —"
"Alright!!!!! Alright!!! That's alright!"
Todd stood up from his seat,
Clint Eastwood style.
He sat next to me.
He took out his bubble gum

and stuck it under the table.
Then he gave me a kiss like a
triple trinitrotoluene gimlet,
extra dry, up,
with an olive of
exaggeration and bazooka,
and I must say he did exhibit
some native *suavité*
when he led me to his component
and I mounted it
and we vavoomed out of
Tacoland
freestyling into heaven
neck and neck with condors and biplanes.
"Jesus, Todd, I didn't know it was gonna
be like this. Why didn't you tell me.
Look, you can see the old neighborhood
from here. See, there's the apartment
building where I grew up on 8811 Dogcatcher
Avenue. There's my elementary school:
Charles Darwin. And there's my panda bear,
the one my mother got rid of when I was
seven. See, there it is, there,
in the incinerator."
The little rapscallion held me tight
and I pounded down destiny
secure with my midnight thrasher

in a shred *de deux*
tandem
an anachronism airborne
happy
and
somebody's
childhood sweetheart.

SALOON

For John Miner

I like cowboys
I like 'em.
Those powdered gauchos of Channel 13
with bullets and justice,
steeds and frontiers.
I was arrested
in my saddle
shoes and donkey
tails and made
beautiful
like my mother.
Saturdays at two were a reliable salvation.
Lengthy Saturdays.
With good-night kisses as valuable
as silver dollars
and The West
tight
on the arm of a man.

BLACK BRA

"Why don't we take off our clothes?"
This changes the course of our lives.
He has too much hair on his body.
He smokes.
I wouldn't be so fatalistic
but he said he was
caught short
so I said ok
I'd pay for everything.

I'm locked in the bathroom
and I'm never coming out.
Seventy years bad luck.
I'm the woman
in the horror
quivering imperiled
clutching her reflection
while something obscene
knocks on the door.
My mother and grandmother
stood on the other side
manipulating:
Open up and forgive them.
Caviling in whispers

about my idiosyncracies.
I'd drown them.
I'd draw the bath
with a heaven of bubbles
and vow:
Someday I'm going to be a
flapper.

The trill of whores
agreeing
Your Face Is Your Fortune
"Try on this & this & this!
What a beautiful body you have."
And in costly bustiers
hose, dangles
scant oodles
of frou frou
in the mirror
of Lili St. Cyr
it's me
and my
dogma.

He undresses himself
so I undress myself.

His kiss
is worse than anything.
It's worse than when my mother
forced me to wear
clothes that I hated.
Puffed sleeves.
I had to go out in the world
like that
in princess collars
long after I was a woman.

There's no such thing as
men.
So why do I continue to buy
these pretty little things?
I can't even imagine.

WAYNE

Why be sixteen
when you could have a tattoo.
After all.
God, you wanted to kick school
and become addicted to a wage.
Tony hired you on afternoons at the garage.
Tony, Joe and Geraldo were burly
and sent you out for submarines.
After an afternoon
of buffing pumps and divorcees in leaking Camaros
Tony'd take you to his hood
and raise it
and let you tremble
before his older, yet Venusian
Lamborghini.
It took an entire week
of scrubbing squeegees
'cross the wet rears
of mollycoddled clientesses
to finally afford
that Sacred Heart of Jesus
sweetening your deltoid.
I saw it, too.
I saw it when you changed your shirt.

I saw your body
beneath a balustrade of white walls,
beneath the galaxy of topless women stacked
atop the tins of antifreeze.
You had the sexiest skeleton.
We looked at each other.
"Employees only beyond this point."

PUBCRAWLER

Another hot summer without a man.
I bustle down to the scrotum bar.
This strobing fan & ice cold 'tender
Make me dream of being bedridden.

KIDDIE SHOWS I USED TO WATCH

My mother lashed me to the
screen
where everything was Black & White
and she turned it on.
Captain Kangaroo had a lap
like a department store Santa.
I was left alone on the couch with
Mighty Mouse and Crusader Rabbit.
Roadrunner, Daffy, Felix, Bullwinkle, Bugs & Rags
leaped into the living
room with soft paws and falsettos while their
villains, forever penned, leered through the incandescent
cage, gnashed their teeth and growled.
I could black it out with a button.
Meanwhile
my mother bellied by
in spike mules and a
snippy bikini
to answer the
door
for some grisly simian
who came to fix her washing machine.
He looked like that scary caricature of a
"stranger" thumbtacked on the

wall of my kindergarten.
They open their car
door
and offer you pomegranate suckers but you
mustn't get in with them.
Through the carefully left
open
crack
in the kitchen
door
I could see my mother posing on a
stepladder and chirping and pointing
the painted toenails of one foot
at her busted wringer;
her Spring-O-Lator dangling mid-air by a strap,
her instep bobbing it
articulately.
I could also see a three-fingered hand
with enormous knuckles,
covered with hair like rusty nails,
grasping a tool.
Porky and Goofy,
beardless and puffy,
stood at the loosed
gate
of our harem,
with red lollipops in their mouths.

THE MAYAN

And in more spectacular
versions she had taken a
Spanish Fly
or was a whore
or used to go steady
with Ricky Gonzalez.
Nobody knew her name
or when.
It looked like La Scala
but it was The Mayan.
All over the walls were
Persephone, Paris and
Clytemnestra
And you know where it is
that little place
up front, on each side of the screen
at the end of the aisle
the Exit
behind
the ancient curtain
purple and undisclosing
as a phantom's cape
Well, it was there
right there,

in that little exit
there was this boy and this girl
and they were making it
and then she got hot
and then she got cold
and they were stuck
yeah, stuck
and the man who takes the tickets
had to call the ambulance
and they had to carry them out like
that, together
in front of everyone
to the hospital
where the doctors had to get them apart.

Oh, man, I hope that never happens to me!
I hoped, when I was 11.
What's "*hot*?" And what's "*cold*?"
There was an entrance
out of the backstage
of being seen but not heard:
Don't run
Don't hold hands with your girlfriend,
and never ask
what does anything mean.

I would have been a dwarf
if it weren't for
Carmen Wilson.
She was cool.
She was 12, carried a purse and was
half-Mexican.
She went to The Mayan every Saturday.
Pre-homeroom
Girls' rooms of the world
tart with
Aquanet, Salems
lore and phantasmagoria
where Carmen would
clue me in:
He phoned her
He told her
He frenched her
He felt her
The ring
the silver chain
the St. Christopher
the tin anklet
with the little tiny heart.
She had met him at The Mayan.
Raoul.
Raoul, oh Raoul.
To have the name of a boy

written on your Pee Chee
with a Lindy
was voodoo.
To have the name of a boy
in your hand
To tuck it under your pillow
and make a wish
to have the name of a boy
was phenomena
way past my bedtime.
To have the name of a boy
gave you
something in the world
willy nilly and extant
and far away from
the irremediable squalor of
childhood.
Carmen
had Raoul
and she emptied his name
like a monomaniacal hosanna
the peak tremulo
of an ungovernable aria
and I listened, listened, listened.

Until one morning bashed open.
Carmen met me

at the lavatory
of the Louis Pasteur
Science Building.
That lavatory
where we carved slugs
out of the tops of cottage cheese cartons
and inserted them into the comb
and Kotex machines.
That lavatory
where every inch of stall
was Marks-a-lotted with the
name of a boy.
Our lavatory,
where we pissed
and construed the simple Id.

And all of a sudden
the door
with the determinant
"girls"
opened
and it was Carmen
in a full-throated absolute:
"It was a blast!"
and she hussied right up
to the communal mirror
so far away I had to

stand on my toes to see
and she pulled down
the big turtle
of her nubile Orlon
and it was there
on her chest
fresh as soap
the gore, the whet, the buss
of lupine buggery:
A boss hickey.
How much longer was I going to
endure this privation!
She got it at The Mayan.
It lasted for two weeks.
All the girls of the
lavatory of the Louis Pasteur
were agog
with envy
and I just about had a cow!
Day and night
I suffered.
I had been introduced to things
polychromatic.
This was the moment when
I discovered my blood.
I was in a girls' room
afoot hexagonals

and I turned the four-foot-one-inch
all of me
to the universe and I demanded to know:
Where's Mine?

Mine
was a second storey
two-bedroom pre-fab
sparkling flocked
salt-and-pepper
wall-to-wall
tissue paper
18-unit construct
painted pink
with a pool
and a fat landlady
in a housecoat and zoris
who only rented to white people
and everybody in all 18
was married with kids
except for Frederika in
number 5
who couldn't have any
and all day long
they had their doors open
and through the screens
you could hear the

TV's howling for their mates
and by nightfall the sobs
and the cops
and *"I'll kill you, bitch!"*
and in front were
dandelions
fenced off with
poodle shit and string
and a deciduous
"For Rent" sign
and in tawny script
above the entry gate:
The Alcatraz Arms.

Mine was a generation
whose mothers had done
daring things
like had inter-faith
marriages.

Mine was the burlesque
with no red light
to tell meter readers
that this was a house
on stilts.

Mine was a cashiered Bardot
in pasties
reading about Jackie Kennedy's wardrobe.
Keeping her husband monogamous
with a nose job from Burbank
and two dim lips
pouted as Pandora's box
with evil.
All the evils of the world
shrew Typhoean screams
to Jesus Christ
because she didn't have a
maid or an XKE.
Where there is sound
there is immortality
so she kept talking.
She stole my little nativity
right out of my cranium
turned me into a reverberation
bewitched me into believing
that phenomena is onomatopoetic
and then fed me my first word:
famine.
To survive
I had to live on my knees
as an ear.
"Look at me when I'm talking to you!"

and I would snap into microphone.
And she would say, *"Dachau"*
and I would say, *"you exist"*
and she would say, *"Hiroshima"*
and I would say, *"you exist"*
and she would say, *"Ethel Rosenberg"*
and I would say, *"you exist"*
and swear by swear
stone by stone
I cradled her monotony
and so remained
benign and could even talk
like all good children
by dint of
ventriloquy.

She couldn't spell or
do simple mathematics.
The biggest satisfaction
of her life was her certitude
that Lena Horne was colored.
She'd had a job once
after the war
pumping gas
till she was fired.
She could cook two things:
ice and Sloppy Joes.

She got herself two husbands
by rolling the cuff of
her short shorts
up over the lip of her ass
and smiling.
No wonder
women matadors
are outlawed in Spain.

Oh, she was mine.
I only knew she was my mother
because my grandmother told me
so.
I don't remember being born.
My grandmother showed me
the photograph of that girl
and that boy
in those chop hair-dos of yesteryear
I'd imagine my mother in a flip
and him in a pompadour
and they could have been
any of those ninth graders
on the lunch pavilion
with all the age and ostentation
of going steady
she in her thick-waisted wedding gown.
It's very hard to trust your ontology

to the word of an old woman
But in those days
if you slept with a man
he married you.

Mine was the roistering brothel
where I was beaten at
age 8
for asking at the
dinner table
what the word *"fuck"* meant.
"Sex," she said,
"was meant to be learned in the gutter."

Brown as the arm of the
Mexican who tooled it
was the strap
with the thick nickel buckle
she carried on her shoulder
day and night
so that she could have me
anytime she wanted.
I ran and ran and
she would chase me
into cobwebs
and finally to the screen door
and it would have been so

easy to lift the latch
and run

But always,
the body that made my body
cut out my tongue.

One day
into the seraglio
came her new man.
She showed him my bound feet
and I called him
daddy.
Daddy was
as big as a door.
He wore green slacks and
a yellow shirt
with a plastic pen holder
in the shirt pocket
that said Drone Spark Plugs.
Soon, he had a belt, too, which at
dinnertime hung over the back of his chair.
We were
a family.

*"When I'm through with you
you'll wish you were dead."*

And they would seize their routine
and I would lunge to the floor
the way I'd been taught
at Benjamin Franklin Elementary
when there was an air raid siren
the last Friday of every month
and you'd quickly hide under the table
with your knees and elbows tucked
into your body and your hands clasped
over your neck to protect your
cortex with your two little
seven-year-old hands
against the hydrogen bomb
when it dropped on you.
Although I had learned *"please"* and
"thank you" from Miss Mary on
Romper Room and how to make
paper ashtrays
there was never a coloring book
on pain.

"Kill her!"
my mother shouted with
each rotation of her arm
and my step-father would say
*"stop crying, I'm not going
to stop till you stop crying."*

I didn't know where to put my little make-believe
because I didn't have a
toy box or a cloak room.
So I searched for the gutter
where you are meant to learn things
and I went down,
down, deeper than you can know
below the world
where they keep the
lockers and the costumes
and I hid in the dark
and waited
until at shame I became a virtuoso.

They whipped till their arms
moaned
and then Onan the paterfamilias
would fall off me
with his belt lying sensitive
over his thigh
and my mother would take her seat
at the head of the table
chafed because she broke a fingernail.
I picked up their marriage
with both my hands
and I resumed my place
in the arrangement.

One inch taller than
my Patty McCoy doll
I asked,
as they taught me,
"May I be excused, please?"
It took me all night
to clear the table
and wash the dishes
and dream
that I had been adopted...
They sat in the living
room with cheap beers and
Bonanza.
I scrubbed the
pans till they shone
to prove we were puritans.
One night
the big white ranchers
were displaced
with Watts.
There was a refrigerator
on fire and people
running with pillows
and television sets.

I stood at the kitchen
door drying the broiler

and watched my mother and step-father
on the porch

screaming:
"Kill the niggers!"
I watched them. I watched them and watched them.
"Kill the niggers!"
my mother scorched
till she was dizzy
and the white dusk
blacked above her
and you got the feeling
of hell.
I watched them, hating together,
like a romance
singing for the annihilation
of human beings
with whoops and the swill of Coors.
This was how they remained
together
how he went to work
and came home
day after day
and made her car payments.

I went to bed.
He went to bed.

But she had her reasons.
She had a migraine
insomnia
constipation
and the vapors.
All night long
my stepfather grew a beard
I dreamt about naked angels
and she lay
with the brothelry and hurly burly
of the Sylvania.
Why was I born?
Why was I born?
Why was I born?
Was all there was
that was hers.

Mine was the shortest girl
at John A. Sutter Junior High.
The very name itself
announced at once that the
primary ethic instructed by the
Los Angeles City School System was
greed.

Mine was the pogrom
instituted by Miss Noyts, the girls' V.P.,

an obese virgin of 59
who made girls
kneel before her
with both knees on
the blacktop
to measure their hem.
If it did not touch the earth
the girl was expelled.
Calibrating appearance
was purely subjective
and statistically
had a lot to do with
Spanish surname.

Mine was the fountain of youth
and the rivers of gold
to which I rose and stood at
attention and pledged allegiance
while over the squawk box
waved amber grain.
I was a patriot.
I believed in my microcosm of
Chop and Sosh which were
gold diggers' dualism
for menials and the propertied elite.
Chop and Sosh.

Mine was the epicenter
of the bird-shit encrusted
soshes, me alone
on a peach bench
amidst the crumpled Cheetos bags
the milk cartons
the apple cores
the wide wale corduroy coats
the pleated white sharkskin snubs
the headbands
the cinnamon stockings
the straw bags
the smart asses
the stupidity
I was completely alone
in the midst of six thousand
sociopathic virgins
wishing I were clothed.

"Marilyn Singleton told me
that you've been telling
the whole school that I
wear falsies" said Nanette Ferrari
digging her fingernails
into my heart.
I'd never heard such a word
as *"False."*

What did it mean, I wonder?
Did it mean the same as *"fuck?"*
and what about the consequences?

This was the lunch bench ritual
like the dinner table ritual
with little soshes about me
with braces and nose jobs
and Marilyn Singleton
the éminence grise
with her arsenal of mohair sweaters.

I was eleven years old
and I had never seen anyone cry.
Why was I the only one I knew
who cried?

*"What are you picking on that
little girl for?"*
Said Carmen Wilson.
She was a greaser.
She was a mean greaser.
I liked greasers. Like me,
their wardrobe was minimalist, too.
Black. Tight. Low.
Black eyes. White Lips. No shit.

With hair high into society
with teenage wrath.

"Nanette Ferrari wears falsies!"
Carmen announced throughout the lunch
pavilion. Then she deflowered
Nanette's blouse with a r-r-r-rip
and then Carmen Wilson —
greaser nonpareil —
proceeded to disgorge Nanette's
Maidenform of reams
of toilet tissue
balled into each cup.
I stopped crying.
Carmen hoisted the evidence
high in her hands
while everyone in the lower-
division lunch period clapped
and then, with inimitable panache
Sutter's most stuck-up sosh
was momentously T.P.'d.
"WHAT'S GOING ON HERE!?!?!?"
said Miss Noyts.
And the world ended.
I grew three inches
as I rose from my little peach bench
and spoke the first words I ever spoke

in my whole life:
"It was her!"
I said, pointing a tall finger at
Marilyn Singleton.
Since I had all A's and Excellences in cooperation,
was in the Athenian
honor society, and volunteered
in the library, the attendance office, the cafeteria
and the math club, my word was as good
as all that glitters.
I quickly learned the power of a lie.
Marilyn Singleton was expelled for
three months, Nanette Ferrari
transferred to a junior high
in a whiter neighborhood
and forevermore
I sat at the table with the Mexicans.

Oh, God, why can't I be Mexican?
I wanna be Mexican.
At the Mexican table
there was a wonderful democracy.
It was the easiest thing in the
world to be enfranchised.
All that was required of
one was to identify all phenomena
as either a phallus or a *puta*

and then vote.
You didn't need a mohair sweater
to be a *puta*.
You didn't need blond hair
to have a phallus.
At the Mexican table
boys and girls sat together
not like at the sock-hop
on Friday after school
where you paid a nickel
to stand in the gym all night
at the wall
watching people
<u>not</u> touch each other,
bodies the regulation two
book-lengths apart.
Mexicans were bards
with exciting and Homeric tales
of phalli and *putas*
in all sorts of
multitudinous and multiplicitous
connivances.
I stopped dreaming about clown collars
and I swapped my apples and
my orange marmalade honey grahams
for priapic *cholos* and humanism.

And Carmen gave me a name: *La Callada.*
"The Quiet One."
And once, I even got to sit next
to Ricky Gonzalez.

Where's mine? Where's mine?
I stood afoot hexagonal tiles
and returned to the communal mirror
face en face
with Carmen's proof that she'd been
to nightfall and back.
"How does that grab you?"
asked Carmen.
"Low, low," I said, although
my heart wasn't really into it.
*"Callada, you've got to come
to The Mayan. You've just
got to. Raoul has the most
boss older brother . . ."*

I did twenty loads of laundry
vacuumed, waxed, dusted,
folded, darned, ironed,
scrubbed, saddle-soaped, scoured,
polished, and shone.
With my Spic and Span and my sponge
I purged the local population

of germs in our household.
I'd commandeer my mop
into hard-to-get embattlements
and jab and squish like a grunt:
"kill, kill!"
and I'd squish, squish
exterminating every
rotten germ
who had ruined my mother's life.
Expiation lay
in the fumes of ammonia
and with a rag and many rubs.
After the genocide
fresh with red hands
I presented myself to my mother
to butt in on her
megalomania.
She was sitting on the
floor of the living room
painting her toenails.
"What do you want?"
And I almost said it:
"Hold me!"

Oh, yeah, if it weren't for
Carmen Wilson, I would
have been infinitesimal

for the rest of my life.
And I quickly learned
the power of another lie:
"Oh, Mommy, dear Mommy,
beautiful Mommy, pretty Mommy,
I'm so glad you're my
Mommy. I wouldn't want to
belong to any other Mommy
but you because you are
the prettiest Mommy. Oh,
Mommy, do you know what?
Marilyn Singleton and her
mother, you know that
live on that big ranch we
drove by in Chatsworth,
and her mother is a
Bluebird leader, you know,
I told you, well they're
going this Saturday
to see Snow White at
the Golden Apple, you know,
by Newberry's and Marilyn
asked me Friday at
lunch if I would like to
go and I have two dollars
saved so could I? Her
mom's driving and will

pick me up at the door
and you can meet her,
so could I?"

What fate wafted through
the screen door then
to grace her vacant
breast, I'll
never know; perhaps it was
the UPS man who had
delivered her a toaster
an hour earlier and looked down
her blouse while she was signing
for it and told her she was
ravishing.
Because she said:
"Alright!"

I posted myself on the
sidewalk in front of
the Alcatraz Arms
one and a half hours
before the expected
arrival of Carmen Wilson
and her mother. Suddenly I saw an
unidentified finned behemoth
barreling up Alcatraz

with the huckstering "Hullaballooer"
blasting platters over KRLA.
It slammed to a skid before me,
and the road cried out loud beneath
the squeal of metal
and the emollient
of Gene Chandler's "Duke of Earl."
The dust blew and the heap
keeled on its chassis,
hull maimed from many
midnight scraps and a
once-in-a-while drunken miscalculation;
with brown chrome, cracked glass,
an unaligned, two-toned
turquoise and whey
bent-bumpered cow
with the Holy Mother of God on the dash
and just at the moment when the massive door towed open
and I pounced onto the front
seat which was covered with
an itchy army blanket and I
heaved the big door fro,
my mother careened out the
gate of the Alcatraz Arms
in time to
catch me
flee

in a 1957 De Soto
with two Mexicans.

If Satan ran an ambulance service
to speed crisp moribunds
to his principality
he'd have a fleet of De Sotos
driven by sirens
the likes of Carmen and her mother
Rosa.

"Hiya Kid!" Rosa said
when we were introduced.
I liked her right away
'cause she was short.
She had peroxided her hair red
and piled it in a massive top-heavy production
of layered curls which had
each been carefully unwrapped
from the brush roller and bobby-pinned in place.
She had man-size lips
and a queen-size *chonch*
squeezed into cut-offs
and corsetted into a tank
topped with the cleavage of
champions.
She had nails that could

open a can of beer.
Why couldn't she be my mother?

She raised her kids on
Gallo and enchiladas
& she grappled that monster De Soto
with her bare feet
reclaiming those *gringo* streets
like don't-you-know-this-is-my-custom-Stutz?
And Rosa would gas that mother
85 up Roscoe Blvd.
burn rubber
rev at pedestrians
honk at slow-pokes
flip off white women
in Brownie leader uniforms
nudge the butt of inattentive
fat-fingered gentlemen in puce Corvettes
and if anybody dared to object
Rosa and Carmen both
flipped the bird together
and then I pitched in
with a psychopathic grimace
and the wrong finger
but then Carmen corrected me
and the next time we spotted
a housewife who looked like

she sold real estate part-time
we'd perch ensemble:
one big one and two little ones!

O, boy
here comes a fart!
and Carmen would spew forth
and we'd crack up, man

and then she handed me
her wilted popsicle
to slurp.
"Feast, Callada."
and I knew it was supurating with
germs. So I sodomized it piously
to prove we were
saliva sisters.
and Carmen and Rosa
sang *"The Monster Mash"*
and *"My Boyfriend's Back"*
and *"Kookie, Give Me Your Comb"*

and then Carmen said:
"Sing, Callada"
but I had never sung
in my life.

I'm sittin' here, la la
waitin' for my ya ya
um hum, um hum
well I'm sittin' here la la
waitin' for my ya ya
um hum, um hum
it may sound funny
but I don't believe
she's comin'
um um, um um

Amber and acrid
was the heat of that
unnoticed afternoon
in a little girl's life
as Rosa docked her hulk
at the parched curb of the
Seaside Oil Station,
just a block away from
The Mayan.
You could even see the Marquee:
"I Was A Teenage Pajama Top
Reform School Vampire From
Outer Space" together with
"Hayley Mills Meets The Blob."
I jumped out
and Carmen and her mother

hugged and kissed
and I had never seen
affection.
As Carmen made for the
door her mother blew me a kiss
"Adios, Callada!"
We waved as the irrepressible
finned behemoth darted
through the school of Fairlanes
and Caddies and Rosa
tooted and winked and backfired
and was gone.

Gas station ladies' rooms
are a universally surrealistic experience.
They are a suffocation chamber of raw concrete
and although they
have built-in containers
for paper towels and
toilet paper, they
never have any. They
always have sanitation tissues
for the seat, however,
which no one ever uses
for that purpose, using
them for toilet paper
and towels instead,

and being there is never
a trash receptacle
the floor is invariably
swamped with soggy
toilet seat tissues
lying in fetal position
like jellyfish
who swam to Santa Monica
to die.
There was only one tiny mirror
hardly big enough for a face
and so high
I had to climb up on the sink
to see.
Carmen's purse was abloom with conspiracy:
Black stockings, garter belt,
a tight, tight skirt,
black hooded Orlon sweater, make-up,
pills, matches, rubbers
and beer.
I didn't like the way it tasted
but I knew it was very grown-up
to enjoy bitterness.
I held my cigarette with my lips
and smoked as I shaved my legs
with Carmen's razor
knowing by this time

tomorrow these tiny little legs
would be razed with welts
as my punishment
because I took my chance
at being young.
Without fear I ratted my hair
till it towered and I
girdered it with spray
without fear I fastened my
hose on my garters
without fear I painted my fingernails green
without fear I pierced my ears with
a sewing needle, hot water and string
without fear I opened the door
of the ladies' room of the
Seaside Oil Station
lit up on Salems
and the whistles of the
boys at the pumps
to whom I blew rings
'cause, man,
I was just so tough.

Everybody was there.
Boys from all over the world.
I'd never seen so many boys.
Truck loads, bus loads, van loads,

woodies and hearses and Impalas
unloading nations
of cute, cute boys.
I was so happy.
Carmen and I trooped to the box
office as if <u>we</u> were there to
see the movie. They were all
in jeans, Pendletons and fluctuating
baritones and they combed their hair
with little black combs they kept in their
back pocket. Even in Carmen's four-inch
stilettos, I was only as tall as an armpit.
I pushed into the prickly swarm; *"Hey, man" "Cool,*
man" "yeah, man" "wow, man" "sheeeeit,
man" "what's happ'nin', man" "qué pasa,
man" dopplered into my consciousness
like pass words I must remember to remember.
Carmen and I paid our dollar twenty-five cents
each and I just knew I would chicken out
but then Ricky Gonzalez walked by me
and said, *"Hello."*

The ticket-taking acne-faced usher
checked me in and checked me out
and tore my ticket in two
and gave me back the other
half to hold in my hand

like a transfer.
The foyer was where the
girls picked out who they wanted.
It was a tropic of boys
and Carmen and I elbowed our
way into the undergrowth
of napes and faces,
shoulder blades and butts
and chests and eyes and wisecracks,
through the agitation
at the concessionary
vollying for bonbons and Gatorade
to a clearing by the
double doors that led
to the sanctuary
where waiting for us
were two gods
who had descended to this place
of buttered Mancini tracks
for the purpose for which gods
had once visited Chichen Itza:
to get girls.
Raoul was 12 and he called
Carmen *"baby."*
They went right away to heaven
leaving me alone with the older god.
God

was a majestic
fifteen enormous years old.
He didn't wear a Pendleton
just his white T-shirt
and despite my education
I decided then and there
that earth's most dazzling ore
was a man's body.
Ponce De Leon died
before he ever found these eyelashes.
God
had on a hat
A Neopolitan organ grinder's hat
with a red feather.
It would have looked
dumb on a dumb kid
but on God. . .
it indicated to me
that he had an intrinsic,
free-thinking bitchenness
deep down in his sensitive soul
underneath that long black hair
and those pink cupid's bow lips
and just the barest adumbration of
a mustache. . .
"Hi!" I said.
"Hi!" he said.

"What's your name?"
"Escamillo."
Escamillo. Escamillo.
Oh, Escamillo.
With the name of a boy in
one hand
and less than half a young life in
the other
I was, all on my own,
ready
And Carmen said,
"Let's go!"

Four spelunkers groping
our way
over the dark side of the
moon, sloshing through
Coke puddles, smuggled beers,
the steady launch of Good 'n Plenty,
popcorn pellets and lumpy feet
which imperiled our very lives,
feeling our way
through the no-man's-land
of the loges.

In the meek phosphoresce
which lit this morbid asteroid

nothing could grow
except youth.

I was next to Escamillo,
very next to him.
In the year that she was
murdered
"Coming Attractions"
was an open coffin
displaying
Marilyn Monroe.
And I laughed.
There was a plot for me
in potter's field
but I didn't know it yet
& I laughed.
I laughed
with the boys
never suspecting
that I, too, would soon be
popping from birthday cakes
smiling at my executioners.

A great thick mask of screams
& intangible fumey joy
plucked the mob
when she took off her clothes

when she stepped into
the white tiled shower
when she opened the faucets
when the spray sparked and stung
when the streams
        pattered her spine
when she held back
        her head and
        closed her eyes and
        opened her mouth and
        let the shower
        touch her tongue

and when the bathroom door was opened
& the curtain was pulled open
& she opened her eyes
& the big blade
& the big man
& the senselessness of all existence
whipped across her stomach
& into her stomach
till the tip hit tile
till his fist could force no further
& she tried to cover her breasts
& she opened her eyes

& the phantom was always indiscernible
& his instrument was full

& her last grasp was the plastic curtain
& its rings snapped when her body slumped
& the nozzle still sprayed hard

& the screams of the theatre crested
& everyone clapped
& the epitaph read:
"Coming soon!"
over the mass grave
of the unknown
woman.

During Bugs Bunny
Escamillo offered me a Jujube
and I took it.
In a precise, calculated,
pre-determined casual manner
he put his arm around my seat
and I wondered how long
it could remain there
before it fell asleep
and he got a charley horse
in his pectoral.
With his free hand

he cocked his brim
back a hair.
Oh, God, I hope my mother
doesn't call the cops!
Like when I was eight
at Alice May's slumber party
two doors down in number 9
when Alice May passed out
her mother's sleeping pills
and then there was a raid
and all the cops found were
dusters and bags
full of little pink girls
fast asleep.

Every seat in the Mayan
was cramped
with pedophilia.

The trick seemed to be
to duck the ushers
who patrolled the aisles
with a flashlight
and who sharply shot
that blinding bang
smack in the faces of the
amoral.

The pair would then beam,
chew Chiclets,
and wait for the
aperture to close.

Escamillo had been in the
ring many times
I guess
because he waited
for the vigilantes
to reach apogee
before he jumped the fence
and then that big boy's mouth
came down on my mouth
and everything in the world transpired
without sub-titles;
and they called the ambulance immediately
and I could hear the big De Soto coming
but I was stuck
yeah, stuck
on the organ grinder
and his horns gored the
screen
and his mass
carried me away like that
in front of everyone
and from that day to this

although I've had to serve
in many prisons
I'm free
beneath the world
in love.

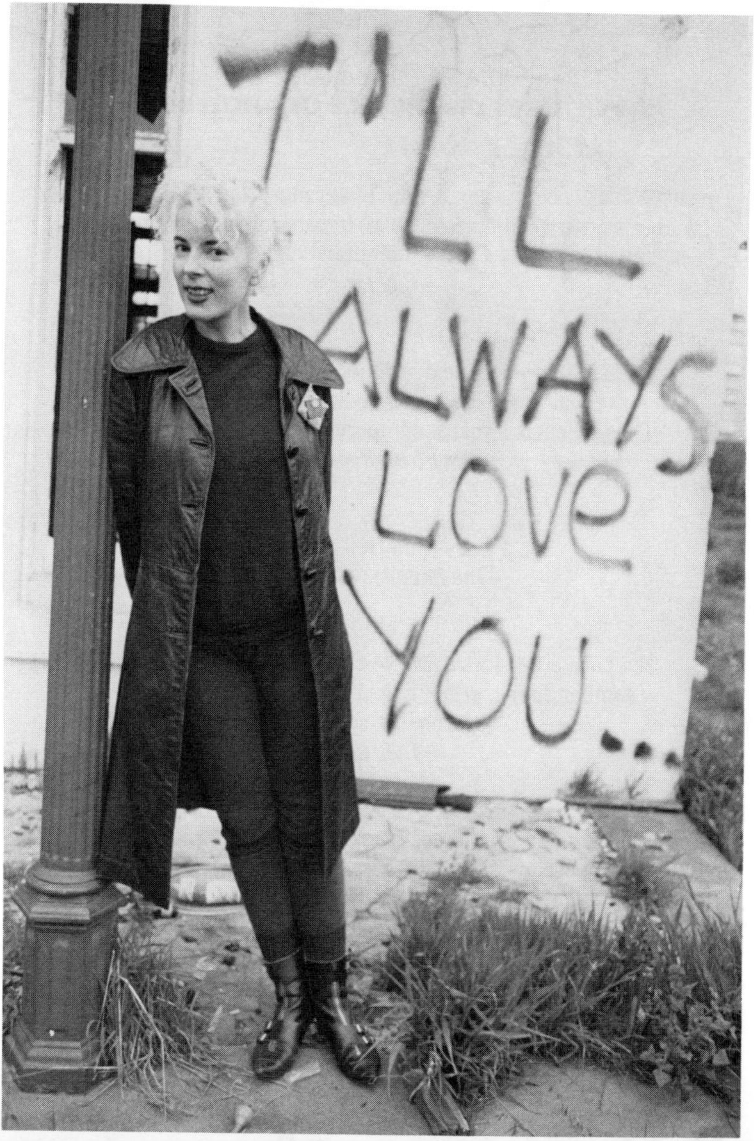

Photo by Peter Milne